Welcome to *The Life of a Fighter*

You are about to enter the first book in *The Life of a Fighter* series—a raw and unfiltered journey through struggle, survival, and the pursuit of hope. This is more than just a story; it is a testament to the strength of the human spirit and the will to keep moving forward, no matter the obstacles.

Life can be brutal. Pain, heartbreak, and betrayal can leave deep scars, making it feel impossible to break free from the past. But this is the story of someone who refused to be defined by suffering. From the grip of child molestation, anger, betrayal, and depression to the fight for healing and purpose, this is a journey of transformation—one fought for and won, step by step.

With each chapter, you will step into the mind and heart of a fighter—someone who faced darkness head-on and refused to let it win. This book is for anyone who has ever felt abandoned, unheard, or trapped by their past. It is not just about surviving—it is about learning to thrive, finding meaning in the pain, and discovering hope even in the most broken places.

You are not alone in your struggles. No matter where you are in your own journey, know that healing is possible, and there is always a way forward.

Let's walk this path together

Heavenly Father,

I come before You with gratitude for every person who opens this book. You know their hearts, their struggles, their dreams, and the battles they have faced—some seen by others and some carried in silence. Lord, as they embark on this journey through these pages, I ask that You meet them right where they are.

May this book be more than words on a page—may it be a source of encouragement, a light in dark places, and a reminder that no battle is fought alone. Let them see that in every hardship, you are present. In every tear, you bring comfort. In every challenge, you provide strength. And in every victory, you deserve the glory.

For those who feel weary, Lord, renew their strength. For those who feel lost, guide them. For those who carry pain, bring healing. And for those who struggle to see hope, restore their faith in Your perfect plan.

Father, I pray that this story stirs something deep within them—a fire to keep fighting, to keep believing, and to keep trusting You. Let them know that no setback is final, no failure defines them, and no battle is bigger than Your power to redeem and restore.

May they finish this book not only entertained or inspired but transformed—strengthened in their faith, emboldened in their purpose, and reassured of the mighty hand that holds them through every storm.

I place this book, its message, and every reader into Your loving hands. May it be used for Your glory and to touch lives in ways beyond what we could imagine.

In Jesus' mighty name,
Amen.

The Fighter's Path

I walk a road both rough and steep,
With wounds too deep for most to see.
Yet step by step, I press ahead,
For the Lord is near—He's where I tread.

The world has tried to break my soul,
To crush my dreams, to take control.
But I was forged in fire and pain,
And by His grace, I rise again.

I've stumbled hard, I've lost my way,
I've fought through nights that stole the day.
Yet even when I felt alone,
His mighty hands still led me home.

I've cried in silence, knelt in prayer,
Poured out my heart, laid my burdens bare.
And in the darkness, through my tears,
He whispered, **"Child, I'm always here."**

Not for glory, not for fame,
Not just to wear a fearless name.
But for the ones who need His light,
Who search for hope in endless night.

For the weary hearts, the broken souls,
The ones who think they've lost control.
For them, I stand, for them, I fight,
To show that grace restores the night.

He is my strength when I grow weak,
The solid ground beneath my feet.
No storm can shake what He has planned,
For I am held in His great hands.

So I will rise, I will endure,
For in His love, my path is sure.
No chains can hold, no fear can bind,
For in my Lord, my strength I find.

Table Of Contents

Chapter 1: A New Beginning

The funeral for Alexander Victory was held on a crisp autumn day, with golden leaves swirling around the cemetery as mourners gathered to pay their respects. The air was heavy with grief, but also with reverence for the life that Alexander had lived—a life marked by hard work, integrity, and devotion to his family and business. As the service began, the eulogy was delivered by a longtime colleague who had worked side-by-side with Alexander for many years. His voice was steady, though there was an occasional tremor that spoke to the sorrow he felt. The eulogy painted a picture of Alexander Victory as a man of principle, someone who had built The Law Office of Victory from the ground up with not just skill but also with a deep sense of morality.

The room fell silent as the speaker recounted Alexander's contributions to the firm, his unyielding commitment to fairness, and his leadership that had inspired so many. The mourners hung on every word, listening intently to the story of a man who had not just been a businessman, but a mentor, a friend, and a father. David Davis stood at the back of the room, his hands clasped in front of him, taking in the tribute to his late boss. Though their relationship had always been professional, David had come to respect Alexander deeply. As he listened, he couldn't help but feel the weight of the loss, not just for the Victory family but for the entire firm.

As the eulogy came to an end, Shawn Victory, Alexander's son, stood at the front of the room, his face composed yet filled with sorrow. He took a moment to gather himself before speaking, and when he did, his voice was steady, though tinged with emotion.

"My father was more than just a businessman," Shawn began. He was my mentor, my guide, and my father. He taught me everything I know about leadership, about integrity, and about what it means to build something that lasts. I know that I speak for my family when I say that his loss is felt deeply. But I also know that he built this firm with a purpose, and it is my responsibility to carry that legacy forward. I promise you all that I will do my best to honor his memory and continue the work he started.

There was a long pause as Shawn stood there, his eyes scanning the room of mourners. His voice cracked for a moment, but he regained his composure quickly. "Thank you all for being here today. Your support means the world to my family and me." The service continued with soft music playing in the background, a moment of quiet reflection for those who had gathered. It was a time to pay respects, to offer a final goodbye, and to contemplate the life of the man they had lost.

Afterward, the procession moved to the cemetery, where the casket was lowered into the ground. The air was cool, and the sound of leaves rustling in the trees created a quiet, mournful backdrop to the ceremony. Shawn stood at the grave, his hands clasped in front of him, his gaze fixed on the casket as it was lowered. David stood a few feet away, his heart heavy with empathy for the new CEO of the firm. Shawn's loss was not just the passing of a father but also the beginning of a new chapter in his life—one that came with immense responsibility.

As the funeral ended, the mourners slowly made their way to their cars, offering their condolences to Shawn and his family. David approached Shawn quietly, unsure of what to say, but knowing that this was a moment where words mattered.

"I'm sorry for your loss, Shawn," David said, his voice filled with genuine empathy. "Your father was a great man. His legacy will live on in this firm and in all of us who had the privilege of working with him."

Shawn looked up at David, his eyes red from the tears that had been shed earlier. A faint smile crossed his face as he nodded. "Thank you, David. It's just so surreal. I keep expecting him to walk through that door at any moment."

David placed a reassuring hand on Shawn's shoulder. "I can't imagine what you're going through. But I want you to know that you're not alone in this. The firm, your family—we're all here for you."

Shawn nodded, grateful for the support. "I'm going to need all the help I can get."

The following week, a small gathering was held at the office to officially welcome Shawn as the new CEO of The Law Office of Victory. It was a somber event, as the staff was still processing the loss of Alexander, but it was also a moment of transition, a chance to honor the future of the firm under Shawn's leadership. The employees had gathered in the conference room, their faces a mixture of grief and curiosity. Some had worked alongside Alexander for decades, and the sense of loss was still fresh in their hearts.

Shawn arrived quietly, his presence commanding attention even in his grief. As he stepped into the room, he paused briefly before making his way to the front. He looked out at the employees who had gathered, many of whom were his father's colleagues and friends. The room was filled with an unspoken understanding that this was a pivotal moment—not just for Shawn but for the future of the firm. He stood at the front, taking a deep breath before speaking.

"Thank you all for being here today," Shawn said, his voice steady but carrying a weight that only those who had experienced loss could understand. "I know that my father's passing leaves a hole in all of us. He was not just a great leader but a great man. His loss is something we'll all carry with us. But I want you to know that I'm here, and I will do everything I can to honor his legacy."

There was a brief pause as Shawn's eyes swept over the room. "I'm not my father. I'll never be him. But what I can do is continue the work he started, uphold the values he instilled in this firm, and make sure that this place remains a beacon of integrity and excellence."
The room was quiet for a moment, and then a soft round of applause echoed through the conference room. It wasn't loud, but it was sincere. The staff understood the weight of Shawn's words and appreciated the sincerity with which he spoke. Shawn wasn't asking them to forget the past; he was simply asking them to move forward with him.

After the brief speech, the event turned into a small reception where employees approach Shawn individually, offer their condolences, and get to know him better as the new leader of the firm. It was quieter than the usual office gatherings, and many people spoke in hushed tones, remembering Alexander and offering words of encouragement to Shawn. David stood near the back of the room, observing the scene. He had seen Shawn in many different settings, but this was different. This was a moment where vulnerability and strength coexisted, where Shawn was stepping into a role he hadn't planned for and trying to fill the enormous shoes left by his father.

Shawn made his way over to David, his eyes tired but filled with resolve. "Thank you for being here today, David," Shawn said quietly. "It means a lot to me."
David gave a reassuring smile. "Of course. You're not alone in this, Shawn. We're all in this together."

The two men shared a moment of understanding before Shawn moved to speak with other members of the staff. It was clear that, while the future of The Law Office of Victory was uncertain, there was hope. Shawn's determination to honor his father's legacy and his willingness to lean on those around him would be the foundation upon which the firm would rebuild.

As the evening wound down and the last of the guests departed, David lingered for a moment. He couldn't help but wonder what the future would hold for the firm, but one thing was certain—the road ahead would be difficult, but with Shawn at the helm, there was hope for the future. The challenges they would face in the coming months were immense, but they would face them together, as a team, united in their dedication to the legacy of Alexander Victory.

David led Shawn through the office, pointing out key departments and introducing him to the employees who were present. It was a quiet tour—more about familiarizing Shawn with the layout of the office than anything else. David noticed how Shawn seemed lost in thought, his gaze occasionally drifting as if he were trying to process everything at once. David had always been practical, but he could tell that Shawn's mind was working on multiple levels—business decisions, personnel issues, and the weight of leading the firm in the wake of his father's passing.

As they walked through the open-plan offices, Shawn asked questions about ongoing projects and the firm's financial standing. It was clear that Shawn's focus was sharp, but there was a weariness in his voice that hinted at the emotional toll the past week had taken on him.

By the time they reached the break room, the tour had taken nearly an hour. David paused, sensing that Shawn might need a moment to process everything. "How are you holding up, really?" David asked, his voice softer now.
Shawn let out a long breath. "It's been a lot. I'm trying to keep my head above water, but it's tough. I never imagined I'd be in this position so soon."

David nodded. "It's not easy. But you don't have to do this alone, Shawn. I'm here if you ever need to talk or get some perspective."

Shawn glanced at him, his expression softening. "Thanks, David. I appreciate that more than you know."

The conversation marked the beginning of a deeper connection between them. Over the next few weeks, David and Shawn spent more time together—working late, discussing the direction of the firm, and occasionally talking about their families. David's daughters, Cariana and Carly, had been busy with their schoolwork and extracurriculars. Cariana had already developed a close friendship with Shawn's daughter, Sara, and the two girls had become inseparable, their shared academic drive creating a bond that seemed unbreakable.

As David settled into his new routine, he could sense the weight of the responsibility on Shawn's shoulders. Shawn had inherited not just a business but also a legacy. It would take time to adjust, and the road ahead was uncertain, but one thing was clear: The Law Office of Victory was in good hands. With David by his side, and the support of the dedicated team that had worked under his father for so long, Shawn was ready to take on the challenges that lay ahead.

It was just the beginning, and the journey would be long—but it was a journey they would face together.

Chapter 2: Struggling Under Pressure

David's workload at the company has intensified over the past few months. He had always been the go-to guy—dependable, meticulous, always willing to take on more. But lately, the pressure has been overwhelming. At first, it was just an extra project here and there, a few more late nights to meet deadlines. But slowly, the work piled up, and with it came the stress. David, who once thrived in the face of challenge, began to buckle under the weight. His once sharp focus began to fade, replaced by a persistent sense of dread and exhaustion. He needed something to cope, something to numb the constant pressure.

That's when the alcohol came in. It started innocently enough, just a drink after work to unwind. But soon, it became a habit—more than just one drink. David found solace in the familiar burn as the alcohol slid down his throat, a brief escape from overwhelming expectations at work and at home. But as the days went on, the amount he drank grew. It wasn't long before it started affecting his ability to function—late mornings, missed meetings, and sloppy presentations. His colleagues began to notice the changes, the once dependable, driven David slipping into someone unrecognizable.

Shawn, his closest friend at work, began to see the decline before anyone else. He had always known David to be the one who kept the team on track, the one with all the answers. But now, Shawn saw his friend stumbling into the office late, his shirt half tucked in, his breath tinged with alcohol. He tried reaching out, tried offering support, but every time he asked if David was okay, David insisted that everything was fine. Still, Shawn couldn't ignore the truth, it was clear that David was spiraling.

"I've noticed you've been off lately, David. Is everything okay?" Shawn asked one morning, as they stood by the coffee machine.
David waved him off, his gaze distant. "I'm fine, really."
But Shawn wasn't convinced. The signs were too obvious. "You know I'm here if you need to talk, right?"

David just nodded, a half-smile plastered on his face, but it didn't reach his eyes. He brushed Shawn's concern aside, unwilling to admit the truth even to himself.

Weeks passed, and the situation only worsened.

David's once impeccable work ethic was replaced by erratic behavior. He started showing up late, or sometimes not at all. His presentations, once crisp and professional, were now riddled with errors. Colleagues began whispering, wondering what had happened to the dependable David. The trust they had placed in him began to erode, replaced with concern and uncertainty.

One afternoon, David stumbled into the office after a long lunch. His eyes were bloodshot, his steps unsteady. The smell of alcohol hung in the air, a stark contrast to the sharp, confident professional everyone had once relied on. He fumbled through a presentation, trying to make sense of the slides before him, but it was clear to everyone in the room—he was not the same person. His thoughts were clouded, his focus gone. It was a low point. His colleagues exchanged uneasy glances, some shaking their heads, others avoiding eye contact. It was evident to everyone but David himself that he was in trouble.

Shawn had seen enough. He pulled David aside after the disastrous meeting, his heart heavy with concern. "This has gone on long enough, David," he said, his tone firm. "You're not just hurting yourself; you're dragging down the team too.

What's really going on?"

David's façade finally cracked. His voice trembled as he confessed, "I don't know how to handle everything anymore. The pressure... it's crushing me." His words were barely above a whisper, but they carried a weight Shawn hadn't expected. For the first time, David wasn't pretending to be fine. He was breaking down.

Shawn placed a hand on his shoulder, trying to offer reassurance. "You don't have to do this alone, man. Let's figure it out together."

But despite Shawn's offer of support, David's downward spiral continued. His drinking grew more frequent, and with it came deeper shame and regret. Each failed attempt to get back on track only made him feel more trapped in the cycle of self-destruction. He couldn't seem to stop himself, and the guilt he felt after each binge only pushed him further into isolation.
His behavior continued to deteriorate. He showed up late, smelling of alcohol, his attitude toward colleagues becoming increasingly abrasive. Shawn tried to talk to him again, but David brushed him off. He was unreachable. Finally, Shawn was left with no choice. He had to give David a final warning.

The company could no longer ignore his behavior.

That night, after an argument with Carrie, David was pulled over for speeding. He was arrested for driving under the influence. It felt like the universe had finally caught up with him. The consequences of his actions were no longer avoidable.

Carrie, frantic with worry, reached out to Mary, who then informed Shawn. Shawn immediately checked the office security cameras, seeing footage of David being arrested in handcuffs. The sight hit him like a punch to the gut. His best friend, someone he had known for years, someone he had once trusted, was unraveling before his eyes. The toll it had taken on both David's career and personal life was clear. And now, Shawn had a decision to make. He knew what had to be done, but it didn't make it any easier.

Shawn rescheduled a crucial company meeting and reluctantly began preparing the termination paperwork. As he stared at the termination letter on his desk, his mind raced with conflicting thoughts. He had watched David transform from a hardworking, reliable colleague into someone unrecognizable. But part of him hoped that this would be the wake-up call David needed to finally confront his demons. Deep down, Shawn felt an overwhelming guilt. He was firing his best friend. Was this the right decision?

David was released from jail later that day, and Shawn called him in for a meeting. When David arrived, his face was a mask of exhaustion and anger. He had already processed what was coming but hearing it from Shawn's lips still hit him like a physical blow.

"The board voted, and they decided to let you go. You'll receive a three-month severance package. You need to get your life together."

David's heart sank. He had seen this coming, but hearing the words spoken aloud made it real. He couldn't believe his best friend, the one person who had always had his back, was the one delivering the blow. Anger flared in David's chest, a hot surge of emotion that he couldn't control. Without a word, he stood up and stormed out of the office, seething with rage. The betrayal cut deeper than the termination itself. How could Shawn do this to him? They had been through everything together—years of friendship, countless late nights working to build the company. And now, it was all crumbling.

As he reached his car, he slammed the door shut, gripping the steering wheel with white knuckles. The frustration and hurt bubbled over, his mind racing with thoughts of how Shawn had failed him. Was this really the board's decision? he wondered. Or had Shawn just grown tired of him?

When David arrived home, the scene was far from a warm welcome. Carrie stood in front of him, her eyes filled with tears and anger. "What the heck are you doing, David?" she demanded. "You disappeared, got yourself arrested, and didn't even think to call. Do you realize what you're doing to us?"

David groaned, rubbing his temples. "I don't need a lecture right now, Carrie. It's been a rough day."

"A rough day?" she snapped. "Every day has been rough for months, and you're the reason why! Your drinking is tearing this family apart. Cariana's grades are slipping, David—she's struggling in school. Don't you see what this is doing to her?"

The mention of their daughter struck a nerve. Cariana had once looked up to him, trusted him, but now, she was scared. She didn't know which version of her stepfather she would get each day, would it be the loving, caring stepdad who helped with her homework, or the angry, drunk stranger who shouted at her mother?

David's anger flared, and he shouted back, "Don't put this on me! I'm doing the best I can. You think I don't know things are messed up right now? I'm dealing with enough without you piling on!"

Carrie's expression softened for a moment, but her voice remained firm. "David, we're all dealing with this. You're not the only one suffering. Cariana is scared—she doesn't know what's going on with you. She used to come to you for help with her homework, and now she's afraid to talk to you because she doesn't know which version of you, she'll get."

David slammed his fist on the table, the noise echoing through the room. "I'm trying, okay? But you're making it worse! Just… leave me alone!" he spat, turning away from her. He stormed to the kitchen, grabbed a half-empty bottle from the counter, and retreated to the basement. The alcohol burned down his throat, numbing the pain for a moment. But it was only temporary. He knew, deep down, that nothing was going to change.

Chapter 3: Crossing the Line

Without a job, David sank deeper into depression and alcoholism. The once-vibrant home became a shadow of what it once was, filled with tension and unease. Cariana, feeling the weight of the household, took on the role of a caregiver for her younger sister. Balancing school, household chores, and childcare, she struggled to keep up with her responsibilities. Late nights of homework often turned into missed assignments, and her tardiness to school drew the ire of her teachers, who, unaware of her home life, showed little sympathy.

One evening, while their mother, Carrie, worked the late shift and Cariana's younger sister remained upstairs, blissfully unaware with music blasting through the floorboards, the unimaginable occurred. Cariana stood at the kitchen sink, washing dishes, exhaustion weighing heavy on her tired bones. The clinking of plates echoed softly in the quiet house, but her mind was too weary to focus. All she wanted was to finish her chores and rest. But David had other plans.

At first, Cariana barely noticed him stumbling into the kitchen, his heavy steps muffled by the sound of running water. The sharp scent of alcohol followed him like a cloud, thick and suffocating. He mumbled incoherently to himself, his words slurred. Cariana tried to tune him out, as she had so often done when he was in one of his moods. But this time, something was different. His behavior shifted in a way she couldn't ignore.

David moved closer, and suddenly, his large hands were upon her. His touch crawled up her back like the legs of a spider, and Cariana froze, a sickening feeling rising in her chest. "Stop it!" she cried out, her voice trembling with fear, but David wasn't listening. His anger, fueled by alcohol, clouded his judgment, and in an instant, he snapped. Without warning, he grabbed her, his grip harsh and unrelenting, throwing her to the cold, unforgiving floor with a force that sent pain radiating through her body.

Cariana screamed, the sound raw and desperate, as she kicked and struggled, trying to break free. But David, consumed by drunken rage, was too strong. His strength far surpassed hers, and his hands gripped her wrists, pinning them above her head as he hissed through clenched teeth, "Shut up, or I'll hit you!" His voice was primal, full of malice. Terror flooded her, but she was powerless.

Her body stiffened as his grip became brutal, his intentions unmistakable. "No!" she sobbed, thrashing against him, but her struggles only seemed to fuel his determination. Her voice faltered, her screams turning into muffled sobs as David tore at her clothing. The sound of her panties ripping echoed in the silence, drowned out only by her cries. He forced himself on her, shattering her innocence and leaving her broken.

When it was over, Cariana lay on the floor, trembling, her body aching in places she didn't know existed. Her spirit, too, had been shattered, leaving her hollow, empty. Tears streamed down her face as she tried to pull herself together, but there was nothing left of the girl she once was. David, however, seemed unfazed by the destruction he had just caused. Coldly, he ordered, "Go clean yourself up."

Cariana dragged herself to the bathroom, each step a painful reminder of what had just occurred. Her mind raced, unable to make sense of what had happened, replaying the horrifying moments over and over. Her body felt foreign to her, no longer her own. She stood under the cold water of the shower, but it did nothing to wash away the filth she felt inside. Minutes later, David appeared at the door, holding out stomach medicine and ointment for the bruises he had left on her. His gesture, as if it could somehow make up for what he had done, only deepened her pain and disgust.

That night, Cariana cried herself to sleep, her sobs muffled by the pillow pressed to her face. The tears wouldn't stop. The horror of it all refused to leave her, and she couldn't find a way to make it go away. The next morning, David spun a web of lies to Carrie, claiming Cariana had fallen while cleaning and injured herself. Carrie, unaware of the truth, believed him without question.

"Stay home for a few days," Carrie said gently. "You need to rest and recover."

Her mother's words, though meant with kindness, only deepened Cariana's anguish. What she truly needed wasn't rest; it was safety, justice, and someone who would believe her. She needed her mother to see through the lies, to understand that something much darker had happened.

In the days that followed, Cariana withdrew further into herself. She barely spoke, her once-bright spirit now clouded by fear and shame. David's presence in the house became a constant source of terror. Every time he came near her, even in passing, the memories of that night would flood her mind, the terror, the helplessness. Whenever he reached out, even if it was just to touch her hair or her shoulder, she would flinch violently. Her body instinctively recoiled, her breath quickening as her heart raced with fear. She couldn't stop it. She couldn't control the response.

She lived in perpetual fear, convinced that at any moment, David might do it again. She kept her distance from him, but the house wasn't big enough for her to escape. Every time he came close, her body reacted, her mind filled with the terrifying possibility that it might happen again.

One afternoon, the family sat in the living room, a moment of false normalcy. David reached over, brushing a strand of Cariana's hair away from her face, as if it were a tender gesture. But Cariana recoiled sharply, her eyes wide with fear, the anxiety seizing her chest like a vice. Carrie noticed her reaction, the way her body trembled.

"Cariana, are you okay?" her mother asked, concern etched across her face.

Cariana's heart pounded, fear racing through her veins. Her gaze flickered to David, who stared back at her, his expression cold, unmoving, and yet full of control. Fear gripped her chest, and she weighed her response carefully. She had to protect herself somehow. If she told her mother the truth, what would happen? Would Carrie believe her, or would she side with David? And even if she did believe her, would it be enough to stop him?

Finally, after what felt like an eternity, Cariana forced a weak smile. "I'm fine, Mom. Just tired."

Carrie hesitated, her brows furrowed in concern, but David's commanding presence silenced any further questions. His gaze was enough to send a message, this was not something they discussed. Cariana's words, though a fragile lie, were enough to deflect her mother's concern, and for a moment, she could breathe again. But inside, Cariana was screaming. She felt trapped, caught in a web of fear and lies, unable to break free. The truth was a burden she couldn't share without risking everything—her safety, her family, and the fragile thread of hope she still clung to.

Yet, amid the silence, amid the pain, Cariana began to long for a way out. She began to crave freedom, the power to take back control over her life. She dreamt of ending the nightmare that had consumed her existence.

Cariana didn't know when or how she would escape, but she could feel the spark of defiance growing inside her. She might not have the strength to leave just yet, but she would find it. She would find a way to reclaim her power and end the suffocating nightmare that had taken over her life.

Chapter 4: The Silent Battle

When Cariana eventually returned to school, she was not the same person she had been before. The once lively and confident girl who used to walk into class with a bright smile was now a shadow of herself. She moved through the hallways quietly, her head lowered, avoiding eye contact with anyone who tried to speak to her. Most noticeably, she distanced herself from Sara, her best friend, the one person she had always confided in, laughed with, and shared everything with.

Sara noticed the change immediately. At first, she thought Cariana was just having a bad day. But as the days turned into weeks, it became clear that something was wrong. Every time Sara approached her, Cariana found an excuse to leave, whether it was needing to finish an assignment, feeling sick, or simply pretending not to hear her. The excuses piled up, and with each one, Sara felt more and more confused.

Had she done something wrong? Had she said something that hurt Cariana without realizing it? The uncertainty gnawed at her, making her restless.

That afternoon, when Sara returned home, her

mother immediately noticed her unusual quietness. Normally, Sara would chatter excitedly about her day, sharing stories about her teachers, friends, and whatever had happened at school. But today, she barely said a word as she sank into the couch, lost in thought.

Her mother sat beside her, concern etched into her face. "Sara, honey, where's Cariana? I haven't seen her in a while," she asked gently.

Sara hesitated before responding, her voice barely above a whisper. "We don't talk anymore."

Her mother frowned. "You don't? Why not?"

Sara shrugged, her chest tightening. "I don't know," she admitted. "She won't talk to me. She just… avoids me."

Her mother studied her for a moment. "Did you do something wrong?"

Sara quickly shook her head. "No, I didn't," she said, though doubt still lingered in her mind.

Her mother reached out, brushing a strand of hair behind Sara's ear. "Then maybe something's going on with her," she suggested. "Have you tried asking?"

Sara sighed. "Every time I try, she pushes me away."

"Maybe try again," her mother encouraged. "She might need a friend right now, even if she doesn't know how to ask for one."

Sara nodded, considering her mother's words. Maybe she needed to try harder.

The next day at school, Cariana was absent from class. As the teacher finished taking attendance, she turned to Sara. "Can you take the attendance log to the office, please?"

Sara nodded and took the sheet. As she made her way down the hallway, she spotted Cariana near the lockers. She hesitated for a second before deciding that this was her chance.

Stepping closer, she called out, "Cariana?"

Cariana looked up, startled, her expression unreadable.

Sara swallowed hard, trying to keep her voice steady. "Did I do something wrong?" she asked.

Cariana's eyes flickered with something Sara couldn't quite identify before she shook her head. "No," she answered softly.

"Then why won't you talk to me?" Sara pressed, concern laced in her voice.

Cariana hesitated, her hands trembling slightly. She glanced around the hallway before reaching for Sara's hand and pulling her toward the restroom. Without a word, she pushed open the door and quickly shut it behind them, making sure no one else was inside.

Sara's heart pounded. She had never seen Cariana like this before—so tense, so afraid.

Cariana kept her gaze on the floor, her breathing uneven as she struggled to find the words. Then, suddenly, tears welled in her eyes, and she let out a quiet, broken sob.

"Promise me you won't tell anyone,"she whispered, her voice shaking.

Sara froze, stunned by the raw vulnerability in her best friend's eyes. She could see the pain, the fear, and the desperate need for secrecy. Whatever had happened, it was serious.

Swallowing hard, Sara nodded. "I promise," she said, even as a sinking feeling settled in her stomach.

Chapter 5: Confessions and Consequences

Cariana's voice shook as she finally spoke, each word heavier than the last. "A couple of nights ago... my stepdad and I got into it over helping with my little sister. He was drunk, going on about needing a break from us. I tried to reason with him, but he snapped. He hit me. Then... he tried to apologize but hit me again. And then he... he raped me," she choked out, her body trembling with the weight of the truth.

Cariana's voice shook as she finally spoke, each word heavier than the last. "A couple of nights ago... my stepdad..." She took a deep breath, struggling to push the words out, the pain too fresh and overwhelming to speak freely.
Sara, sitting beside her, watched her with concern, her heart aching for her friend, but she stayed silent, giving Cariana the space to share what she could.
Cariana's hands trembled as she wiped her eyes. "At first, I didn't even notice him stumble into the kitchen. He was drunk, like always, but this time... I don't know, something felt different." Her voice cracked, and she lowered her gaze, unable to meet Sara's eyes.

"The smell of alcohol hit me like a wall," Cariana continued, her breath hitching. "He was mumbling to himself, saying things I couldn't even understand. I tried to ignore him, tried to stay out of his way, but he came closer." She paused, swallowing hard. "I froze. When he touched me, it felt wrong. I tried to push him away, but he was stronger. His hands... his hands were everywhere."
Tears welled in Cariana's eyes as she choked on the words. "He... he grabbed me. Pulled me down. Threw me on the floor. I couldn't breathe. It all happened so fast. I was trying to fight back, but... I couldn't. He's so much stronger than me. And I... I didn't know what to do."

Cariana's voice broke as she whispered, "I screamed. I begged him to stop. I told him, 'Stop it, please!' But he didn't care. He told me to shut up or he'd hit me. I couldn't do anything. He was so mad... so angry. His grip was like iron, and I couldn't move, couldn't escape."

Sara felt a cold wave of terror rush over her as she saw how much pain her friend was in. She wanted to say something, to comfort her, but she knew that words couldn't fix this. She just stayed quiet, her heart breaking as Cariana spoke, her eyes wide with distress.

Cariana covered her face with her hands, wiping away the tears, but the sobs didn't stop. "He made me feel like it was my fault, like I deserved it. He told me no one would believe me, that no one would care. And now I can't stop hearing his voice, telling me I'm worthless, telling me I'm nothing."

Cariana's hands shook as she touched the bruise on her cheek, a sickening reminder of what had happened. "I can still feel his hands on me, Sara. It makes me feel disgusted. So betrayed... I don't know what to do. I feel like I can't breathe. Like I'm not even... me anymore."

She broke down, crying harder, her shoulders shaking as she hugged herself tightly. "Why did this have to happen? Why did he do this to me? I just... I don't know how to live with this. I don't even know how to go on anymore."

Sara's heart shattered, and without a second thought, she pulled Cariana into her arms, holding her close as they cried together. She didn't have any answers, didn't know what to say, but she wanted her friend to feel like someone cared, like she wasn't facing this darkness alone.

"I'm so, so sorry,"

Sara whispered, her voice thick with emotion. "You're so strong for sharing this with me, Cariana. I'm here for you. I promise. We'll get through this together. You're not alone."

Sara pulled back slightly, her eyes full of concern and love as she met Cariana's tear-filled gaze. "How about coming to Bible study with me tonight? We can just sit at the back. You don't have to talk to anyone. Sometimes just being there can help. You don't have to be alone in this."

Cariana shook her head, her face crumpling with shame. "I can't. I feel too dirty, Sara. Too uncomfortable. I can't be around anyone right now. I'm not… I'm not the same. Not after what happened."

Sara nodded, her understanding clear. She reached for a paper towel and gently handed it to Cariana, who wiped her tears with trembling hands. "It's okay," Sara said softly, her voice steady despite the heaviness she felt inside. "You don't have to do anything you're not ready for. Just know that I'm here for you. Whenever you're ready, I'll be by your side. No matter what."

Cariana stared down at the paper towel in her hands, her eyes vacant. Her body shook with sobs that refused to stop. Sara didn't rush her to speak, didn't try to fix everything in that moment. Instead, she just stayed by her side, quietly, offering the only comfort she could.

That night, after Sara left, her mother was waiting for her in the kitchen. Her face was full of concern, the unease in her eyes impossible to miss.

"Did you talk to Cariana?" her mother asked gently. Sara hesitated. She knew she couldn't tell her everything. Not yet. She had promised Cariana she would keep her secret, that she would be there for her, and breaking that trust felt too painful. But it weighed on her, the knowledge that Cariana's suffering was so much deeper than anyone knew. "Yes, ma'am," Sara replied softly. "But she said I didn't do anything wrong."

Her mother's brows furrowed as she studied her daughter. "Is that all she said?"

Sara swallowed hard, her heart pounding. She wanted to tell her mother everything—how Cariana had been hurt, how she was in so much pain. But she had made a promise and breaking that promise would feel like betraying Cariana. The burden of it all pressed down on her chest, leaving her uncertain of what to do next.

"She just... she's going through a hard time," Sara said, her voice barely above a whisper.
Her mother sighed, reaching out to tuck a loose strand of hair behind Sara's ear. "If she's in trouble, you need to encourage her to get help. Secrets like these only make the pain worse. You don't have to carry it alone, sweetie."

Sara nodded, but guilt gnawed at her insides. What if Cariana needed more help than she could offer? What if something happened to her? She stared down at her hands, feeling the weight of the secret she was holding, unsure of whether keeping it would protect her friend—or make everything worse.
Lying in bed that night, Sara whispered a prayer. "God, I don't know what to do. Please help me. Help Cariana. Show me the right thing to do." Tears slipped down her cheeks as she clutched her pillow, feeling the unbearable weight of silence.

Chapter 6: Bearing the Burden of Truth

The weight of Cariana's words hit Sara like a tidal wave. She had never felt so helpless in her life. That evening, she tried to focus on getting ready for Bible study, but the image of her friend's tearful face haunted her. She felt overwhelmed with the responsibility to help but didn't know where to start. She prayed, asking God for guidance and for a way to comfort her friend.

Bible study that night began with the usual opening prayer, but Sara felt something stirring in her heart as the pastor began to speak. His words seemed to resonate deeply with the turmoil she was feeling. "Let us turn to 1 Timothy 6:12," the pastor said, "which tells us, 'Fight the good fight of faith, lay hold on eternal life, whereunto thou art also called, and hast professed a good profession before many witnesses.'"

The pastor continued, his voice growing stronger with each word, "We all go through battles that test our faith. Sometimes those battles are visible, but often they're fought in silence, where only God sees the depth of our struggle. But remember, God doesn't call us to fight alone. He equips us with faith and the promise of eternal life to sustain us. Even in the darkest times, we have something worth fighting for—a purpose that transcends our present pain."

He paused, scanning the room before adding, "This Fighter conquered and defeated all His enemies and even death. This Fighter now sits at the right hand of God the Father. His name is Jesus the Christ, God's Son.

Look at your neighbor and say, 'The Life of a Fighter.'"

As the congregation echoed the phrase, Sara felt chills run down her spine. It was as if the pastor was speaking directly to Cariana's situation, to the despair that had taken root in her friend's heart.

The pastor's voice intensified, "There are moments in life when circumstances spiral out of control. But that doesn't mean you're defeated. Don't let the enemy convince you that you've been overcome. With God, you hold the power to rise above any challenge or heartbreak. Even in our weakest moments, God's strength prevails. Remember Philippians

4:13: 'I can do all things through Christ who strengthens me.' It's not our own power that carries us, but His."

The pastor went on, "Sometimes fighting means standing firm against what is wrong. We must put our trust in the Lord, just as God's son trusted unwaveringly in His Father. There are countless souls suffering— many are weighed down by depression, mistreatment, betrayal, rejection, and isolation. We must be ready to be vessels of God's word, to be a light of hope in someone else's darkness. Remember Jesus' words in John 8:12: 'I am the light of the world. Whoever follows me will not walk in darkness but will have the light of life.' God will never let you face a battle without equipping you to overcome it. He parted the Red Sea for Israel, knowing He would forge a path forward."

Sara's eyes welled up as she listened. It was like the pastor was describing Cariana. The message seemed to provide an answer to the prayer she had spoken earlier. She found herself silently thanking God for the pastor's words.

The pastor continued, "Know that the battles you face are not without purpose. They serve to strengthen your faith, sharpen your character, and teach you to trust in God's unwavering guidance. When the weight of life feels overwhelming, remind yourself that you are never alone—God walks with you through every storm.

As Isaiah 41:10 (KJV) declares, 'Fear thou not; for I am with thee: be not dismayed; for I am thy God: I will strengthen thee; yea, I will help thee; yea, I will uphold thee with the right hand of my righteousness.' Let your trust in Him become your anchor when everything else is uncertain.

Remember, even in moments of weakness, God's strength is made perfect. As 2 Corinthians 12:9 (KJV) says, 'My grace is sufficient for thee: for my strength is made perfect in weakness.' Allow yourself to lean into His power and let it be the force that carries you forward. Encourage others who are struggling to see beyond their current pain and recognize the hope that lies ahead. Jesus Himself said in John 16:33 (KJV), 'These things I have spoken unto you, that in me ye might have peace. In the world ye shall have tribulation: but be of good cheer; I have overcome the world.' You are more resilient than you think, and with God and His Son Jesus, there is always a path to victory.

Don't just wait for change—be an instrument of change. Use your voice to uplift, your actions to inspire, and your faith to light the way for those in darkness. Step into each day knowing that your courage and faith have the power to transform not only your life but the lives of those around you. Embrace your divine purpose and walk forward with unwavering strength and boldness." The pastor then invited, "If everyone can bow their heads and raise their hands, I ask those who need strength to stand up, be bold, and resist the spirit of fear and heaviness. Raise your hand now."

Sara raised her hand, tears streaming down her face as she felt a surge of hope. The pastor began praying for those with their hands lifted, " "Lord, I pray for every individual who has raised their hand in faith. I come against every hindrance that seeks to obstruct the reception of Your word. You alone understand the burdens they bear, the struggles they endure, and the strength they require. Grant them courage, O Lord, that they may stand unwavering in the face of adversity. Remove all doubt and disbelief, and teach them to intercede not only for themselves but also for those who are in need of advocacy and support."

The pastor's prayer continued, "Heavenly Father, as declared in 2 Timothy 1:7, You have not given us a spirit of fear, but of power, love, and a sound mind. Enable them to walk in the fullness of Your power, to be steadfast in Your love, and to remain resolute in faith. Bestow upon them wisdom, peace, and endurance. May they learn to trust in

Your divine providence through every trial, recognizing that challenges serve as opportunities for growth in grace and perseverance. Transform their struggles into testimonies and their pain into purpose. To You be all the glory and honor, now and forevermore. In the mighty name of Jesus Christ, Amen."

After the service ended, Sara lingered in her seat, deep in thought. She knew what she had to do. She approached her mom that night and confessed, "I didn't tell you the whole truth. I made a promise to Cariana not to say anything, but after the pastor's message, I feel I have to share what's been going on."

Sara recounted everything—how Cariana's stepdad had assaulted her, the abuse she had endured, the responsibility she felt for her little sister, and her thoughts of suicide. Sara's mom listened intently and responded with understanding, "You did the right thing by telling me, Sara. We have to help Cariana. Tomorrow, we'll go to the school and speak with the principal."

Chapter 7: A Cry for Help

As Sara and her mom pulled into the school parking lot the following day, Sara's eyes immediately landed on Cariana. Her friend was trudging toward the restroom, her shoulders slumped and her steps dragging as if she carried an unbearable weight. A chill of dread crept over Sara. Something was terribly wrong.

"Cariana!" Sara called out, her voice trembling with concern. But Cariana didn't respond. She didn't even turn her head. Her gaze was vacant, far away, as if she wasn't really there at all.

A knot of anxiety twisted in Sara's chest. Without a second thought, she unbuckled her seatbelt and bolted from the car, sprinting toward the restroom. She pushed the door open just in time to see Cariana lifting a handful of pills to her lips.

"Cariana, no!" she screamed, her voice raw with panic. But it was too late. The pills disappeared down Cariana's throat, and within seconds, her face contorted in pain and despair. Her knees buckled as she slumped against the wall, her breath coming in ragged gasps.

Sara's heart pounded wildly. She had to get help. Now. She turned and ran as fast as she could down the hallway, her voice rising in frantic desperation.

"Help! Someone help! Cariana overdosed!"

The school nurse, alerted by Sara's cries, rushed into action. Within moments, she was at Cariana's side, quickly administering Narcan in a desperate attempt to counteract the overdose. Cariana's breathing was shallow, her body weak and unresponsive.

Sara stood frozen in the doorway, tears streaming down her cheeks. She could barely comprehend what had just happened—the horrifying reality that her best friend had tried to end her life.

The sound of sirens pierced the air, growing louder with each passing second. Paramedics rushed into the restroom, their movements swift and practiced. Cariana was carefully lifted onto a stretcher, her body limp.

Sara followed closely behind as they wheeled her outside. The paramedics worked quickly, stabilizing her as best as they could before loading her into the ambulance.

As the ambulance doors closed, Sara whispered a trembling prayer.

"Please, God. Don't take her. Please don't let her die."

The hospital was a blur of flashing lights and hurried footsteps. Cariana lay motionless in a hospital bed, her face pale against the stark white sheets. She was alive, but barely. The overdose had been a close call, and though she had survived, the road to healing would be long and painful.

She wasn't just fighting for her physical health. She was fighting to reclaim the shattered pieces of herself.

The police arrived not long after, their presence heavy and foreboding. Their questions were sharp, relentless.

"What happened?" "Did she say anything beforehand?" "Do you know what led to this?"

Each question felt like a weight pressing down on Sara's chest, making it harder to breathe. She swallowed; her voice shaky as she recounted the moments leading up to the overdose.

"I saw her walking toward the restroom. She looked...gone. Empty. I knew something was wrong. When I ran in, she already had the pills in her hand. I screamed for her to stop, but she took them anyway. Then she collapsed."

The detectives exchanged glances, their expressions darkening.

"Did she mention anything about why she did it?"

Sara hesitated, her heart pounding. She wiped her tear-streaked face and took a shaky breath before answering. "Yes. She told me... she said she was tired of pretending everything was okay. That no one really saw how much pain she was in. She felt like she couldn't escape... that no one could help her."

Sara hesitated before she continued, her voice breaking. "She told me her stepdad...he raped her. She said she couldn't take it anymore. That she felt trapped, like there was no way out."

The officers nodded grimly, jotting down notes before continuing.

"Where's her father?" one of them finally asked.

Sara hesitated. "He... He's on his way."

Moments later, David arrived. His face was tight with worry, his steps urgent. But before he could reach Cariana's room, two officers stepped forward, blocking his path.

"David Reynolds?" one officer asked.

"Yes," he answered, confusion flickering across his face.

"You're under arrest for assault."

Gasps filled the hallway as the officers grabbed his arms and began cuffing him.

Carrie, Cariana's mother, had just arrived. She froze in place, her eyes wide with shock.

"What?" she breathed, shaking her head. "No. No, this can't be happening."

David remained silent, his face expressionless, as if he had already accepted his fate.

Carrie's shock quickly turned to rage.

"Why, David?" Her voice cracked, raw and trembling with pain. "I trusted you!"

She lunged toward him, fists clenched, but the officers held her back. She let out a guttural scream, a sound filled with anguish and betrayal.

It was a scream that reached deep into the past, pulling up memories she had tried so desperately to bury.

Her world was unraveling, thread by thread.

As social workers arrived, they gently explained that her younger daughter would be placed into protective custody until the investigation was complete. The weight of those words crushed her.

She had always sworn she would protect her children. She had promised herself she would keep them safe. But now, her daughter lay in a hospital bed, broken and scarred, and another was being taken away.

She had failed them.

As she stood in that hospital room, staring at her daughter's fragile body, Carrie didn't know if she would ever forgive herself.

But one thing was certain, this was only the beginning of the battle. And she would fight. No matter what it took, she would fight for her daughters.

Chapter 8: A Mother's Regret

When she walked into Cariana's hospital room, Carrie's breath hitched, her pulse quickening at the sight of her daughter. Cariana lay motionless, her frail body swallowed by the stiff white sheets, her dark, vacant eyes fixed on the ceiling as if the world had faded beyond her reach. Machines beeped softly, a rhythmic reminder of life's fragile hold, but her daughter looked anything but alive.

Carrie's hands trembled as she reached for the chair beside the bed and sank into it, her voice breaking as she whispered, "Sweetheart, I'm so, so sorry."

Cariana didn't move.

A lump formed in Carrie's throat, thick and suffocating, but she forced herself to speak. She had spent years burying her past, locking it away like a shameful secret, but now... now there was no hiding.

"When I was your age, I promised myself I would never let my children go through what I did. But... it happened anyway." Her voice cracked, the weight of her confession pressing down on her chest like an unbearable weight.

She exhaled shakily, gripping the bed rail as she fought against the fear clawing at her insides.

"My grandfather, uncle, and cousin... they molested me." The words burned like acid, each syllable reopening wounds that never fully healed. Even after all these years, speaking them aloud felt like stripping herself bare, exposing the scars she had tried so hard to hide.

"It started when I was eight years old and didn't end until I was fourteen. I felt so numb, Cariana. I didn't know how to make the pain go away. There were nights when I didn't want to live anymore, just like you."

Her voice broke on the last words, the weight of shared agony stretching between them like an invisible tether.

Cariana still didn't move. Her expression remained blank, her body curled slightly toward the window, her hands clenched into small, fragile fists. The only sign of life was the slow, rhythmic rise and fall of her chest.

Tears welled in Carrie's eyes as she reached for her daughter's hand, desperate for some connection, but Cariana flinched and pulled away, curling further into herself, as if shrinking from the world.

Carrie swallowed the sob that rose in her throat, pressing her hand against her chest as if she could hold her breaking heart together.

"I thought I could protect you," she choked out. "But I failed. And I'm so, so sorry. I was too blind to see the danger right in front of me. I should have kept you safe. I should have known something was wrong."

Her shoulders shook as she leaned closer, her words breaking under the weight of her grief.

"Please, forgive me. I love you more than anything in this world, and I would give anything to take this pain away."

But Cariana remained silent. No flicker of recognition. No reaction. Just emptiness.

The silence between them stretched, thick and suffocating. Carrie's heart splintered, her tears falling unchecked as she watched the hollow, faraway look in her daughter's eyes. It was as if Cariana had retreated to a place Carrie couldn't reach—a place where the pain was louder than anything else.

Carrie nodded slightly, though Cariana wasn't looking. With a deep, shuddering breath, she pushed herself up from the chair. Her legs felt weak beneath her as she took slow, hesitant steps toward the door, each movement heavy with the crushing weight of failure.

At the doorway, she turned back one last time, hoping, praying for even a flicker of acknowledgment, a blink, a shift—anything.

But Cariana remained still.

Carrie felt like her heart was caving in, the ache inside her so deep it felt like an abyss. The air in the sterile hospital room seemed colder, heavier, pressing down on her shoulders like the guilt she carried.

As she stepped out into the hallway, the sterile hospital air felt suffocating, pressing against her like the shame and guilt she carried. She barely noticed Sara standing there until her friend reached out, concern and understanding etched in her eyes.

"Go ahead," Carrie whispered, her voice fragile, barely audible. "Maybe… maybe she'll talk to you."

Sara nodded gently, squeezing Carrie's arm in silent reassurance before stepping into the room.

Carrie watched as her friend crossed the threshold, the door closing softly behind her.

Alone in the hallway, Carrie wrapped her arms around herself as a sob escaped her lips. She walked forward, each step dragging like she was wading through quicksand, the emptiness following her like

a shadow, her chest tight with the crushing guilt of
a promise she hadn't been able to keep.

Chapter 9: The Power of Faith

Sara visited Cariana every day, refusing to let her friend slip away into the darkness. She would sit by Cariana's bed, sometimes in silence, sometimes reading scripture aloud, her voice tender and full of love. She talked about the pastor's recent message on "The Life of a Fighter," hoping the words would stir something deep within Cariana.

"You're still here for a reason," Sara would say, her voice soft but firm. "God isn't done with you yet."

One verse she kept coming back to was Psalm 34:18: "The Lord is close to the brokenhearted and saves those who are crushed in spirit." She would share it again and again, as though repeating it could somehow fill the cracks in Cariana's heart. "You are not alone in this," she whispered, her eyes shimmering with tears. "I'm here with you, and so is God. You are loved, Cariana, and you are stronger than you realize."

Day by day, Sara's compassion and unwavering presence began to reach through the darkness, offering a glimmer of hope where there had only been despair. Cariana still struggled with overwhelming emotions, but the love surrounding her made her start to believe that healing might be possible. There was still a long journey ahead, but in those quiet moments, she felt a tiny spark of life reignite—a flicker of hope she hadn't thought possible.

As she gained strength, Cariana found herself facing an unknown future. Leaving the safety of the place where she had been recovering filled her with anxiety. What would she be walking back into? Could she truly move forward from her past? Sara, sensing her unease, took her hand and gently reminded her, "Isaiah 26:3 says, 'Thou wilt keep him in perfect peace, whose mind is stayed on thee: because he trusteth in thee.' Cariana, we will fight this together. Keep your mind stayed on the Lord. When you start getting overwhelmed, and imaginations start going over and over in your mind, we will cast them down. 2 Corinthians 10:5 says, 'Casting down imaginations, and every high thing that exalteth itself against the knowledge of God and bringing into captivity every thought to the obedience of Christ.' Say this scripture over and over in your mind."

Cariana smiled faintly, her heart swelling with gratitude. "Thank you, Sara. See you later. Love you."

When Cariana left, she went to stay with Sara's family for a little while. They welcomed her as if she had always been part of them, surrounding her with warmth and encouragement. It was a stark contrast to the emptiness she had felt before. The laughter, the prayers before meals, the constant reminders of God's love—i2t all began to chip away at the walls she had built around her heart.

During this time, Sara took her to the ministry more often. Cariana immersed herself in the Word, soaking in its truths like water in a parched land. She began journaling, writing down scriptures that resonated with her, and reflecting on what God was speaking into her life. She attended Bible studies and found solace in worship, feeling a connection to God she had never fully experienced before.

She also started opening up in ways she never thought possible. Late-night talks with Sara, heartfelt conversations with Sara's parents, and the gentle guidance of the ministry leaders helped her realize that she was not alone. Others had walked through their own valleys and found restoration. Hope was no longer just an abstract concept—it was becoming real.

Through prayer, worship, and the love of those around her, Cariana slowly began to experience the healing power of faith. She was learning to release the pain, to surrender the burdens she had carried for so long, and to trust that God had a plan for her life. The past still lingered, but it no longer held the same power over her. Each day, she walked forward, one step at a time, knowing that she was not walking alone.

God was leading her into a new beginning.

One night, however, Sara found herself overwhelmed. The weight of everything—Cariana's healing journey, her own struggles, and unspoken fears—pressed heavily on her heart. Everyone in the house had gone to bed early, but she couldn't sleep. She felt restless, suffocated by the silence. Needing to clear her head, she grabbed her mother's car keys and slipped out the door, deciding to take a drive through a quiet neighborhood.

As she drove, her mind raced with thoughts, doubts, and anxieties. Her phone buzzed on the seat beside her, and without thinking, she reached down to pick it up. In that split second, she felt a sickening thud against the car. Her heart leaped into her throat. Panic surged through her veins as she gripped the wheel tightly, her breathing rapid and unsteady.

Had she hit someone? Or something? She didn't know. Fear gripped her so tightly she felt paralyzed. She didn't dare stop. She couldn't. Instead, she pressed her foot on the accelerator and kept driving, her hands trembling. The thought of turning around and facing whatever had happened was too terrifying. Maybe it was just an animal, she told herself. Maybe it was nothing at all. But deep down, she wasn't sure.

By the time she got back home, her hands were still shaking as she turned off the ignition. She sat there for a long moment, staring at her reflection in the rearview mirror, her eyes wide with fear and guilt. She wanted to believe it was nothing, to push the thought away, to pretend it had never happened. So, she took a deep breath, wiped the sweat from her palms, and stepped inside the house as if everything was normal.

But the weight of what she had done—or what she might have done—settled deep in her chest, refusing to let go.

Chapter 10: The Pastor's Message

He scanned the congregation, his eyes filled with warmth and understanding. "Faith and perseverance are the foundation of a victorious life. Every trial and temptation refines us, shaping our character and deepening our trust in God's promises. No matter how difficult the journey, we are reminded, *'I can do all things through Christ who strengthens me'* (Philippians 4:13, KJV). Some prayers are answered through seasons of sorrow, moments of near surrender, and trials that seem unbearable—but in the end, every struggle will prove worthwhile. Often, before God leads us to divine opportunities, we must endure great disappointments. Regardless of your past pain or present challenges, rise with courage, wipe away your tears, and choose to worship and praise Jesus with joy."

The pastor's voice grew stronger, filled with encouragement. "Life's trials are not meant to destroy you but to develop you. God sees every tear, hears every prayer, and knows every burden you carry. The very pain you're walking through may be the preparation for the breakthrough you've been praying for. *'My brethren, count it all joy when ye fall into divers temptations'* (James 1:2, KJV), for the testing of your f He scanned the congregation, his eyes filled with warmth and understanding, as if he could see the silent struggles etched in the hearts of those before him. His voice carried both tenderness and authority as he spoke.

"Faith and perseverance are the foundation of a victorious life. Every trial and temptation refines us, shaping our character and deepening our trust in God's promises. No matter how difficult the journey, we are reminded, 'I can do all things through Christ who strengthens me' (Philippians 4:13, KJV).

He let the verse sink in, allowing the weight of its truth to settle in the room before continuing.

"Some prayers are answered through seasons of sorrow, moments of near surrender, and trials that seem unbearable. It is in those times, when hope feels distant, that God is often doing His greatest work. Before He opens doors to divine opportunities, He first prepares us—sometimes through disappointments that shake our very foundation. But hear me today: No matter your past pain or your present struggles, do not lose heart. Rise with courage, wipe away your tears, and choose to worship and praise Jesus with joy. For your suffering is not in vain—it is the preparation for something greater."

The pastor's voice grew stronger, rich with conviction, as he stepped forward, sweeping his gaze across the congregation.

"Life's trials are not meant to destroy you but to develop you. God sees every tear that falls in the quiet of the night. He hears every whispered prayer, even those too painful to speak aloud. He knows every burden you carry, even the ones you try to hide behind a smile. The very pain you're walking through may be the preparation for the breakthrough you've been praying for. 'My brethren, count it all joy when ye fall into divers temptations' (James 1:2, KJV), for the testing of your faith produces patience, endurance, and strength. What the enemy intends for evil, God can turn around for good. Do not be discouraged, for even in the valley, He is working all things together for your good."

A quiet wave of agreement rippled through the congregation—heads nodded, eyes brimmed with tears, hands lifted in surrender.

"You are not forgotten. You are not abandoned. The same God who created the heavens and the earth, the One who numbers the stars and calls them by name, knows you intimately and loves you deeply. He has counted the very hairs on your head. He has seen every moment of your life—every triumph, every failure, every wound, every prayer. And still, He calls you His beloved. 'You are fearfully and wonderfully made' (Psalm 139:14, KJV), and His plans for you are greater than anything you can imagine.

He paused, allowing the words to settle like a balm over wounded hearts. Then, with renewed passion, he declared:

"Jesus is the author and finisher of your faith. He does not leave His work unfinished. If you are still in the midst of the storm, trust that He is not done writing your story. What He has started in you, He will surely bring to completion. Do not give up now. Hold on. Keep the faith. The enemy may have whispered lies that you are too broken, too lost, too unworthy—but I tell you today, you are victorious in Christ. Your breakthrough is coming. Your testimony is being written. And soon, you will stand and declare, 'Look what the Lord has done!'"

A hush fell over the room—then a swell of amens, of tears, of hands raised in surrender. The presence of God was unmistakable. Hope had taken root in weary hearts. The battle was not over, but faith was rising. Victory was near.

Faith produces patience, endurance, and strength. What the enemy intends for evil, God can turn around for good. Do not be discouraged, for even in the valley, He is working all things together for your good."

The pastor's words resonated, stirring hearts across the room. "You are not forgotten. You are not abandoned. The same God who created the heavens and the earth, the One who numbers the stars and calls them by name, knows you intimately and loves you deeply. *'You are fearfully and wonderfully made'* (Psalm 139:14, KJV), and He has a plan for your life greater than anything you can imagine.

Chapter 11: Salvation and New Beginnings

The pastor then invited those who felt called to rededicate or give their lives to the Lord to raise their hands. Among the hands raised was that of Cariana, a young woman who had come to the service feeling the weight of life's burdens. Her hand trembled slightly, but she felt an undeniable urge to respond. She and a few others stepped forward as the pastor asked them to come to the altar.

"The purpose of salvation," the pastor began, "is for us to be reconciled to God and receive the gift of eternal life in heaven. To achieve this, we must accept Jesus Christ as our Lord and Savior."

Opening his Bible, the pastor read Romans 10:9-10: "That if thou shalt confess with thy mouth the Lord Jesus, and shalt believe in thine heart that God hath raised him from the dead, thou shalt be saved." He looked out at those who had come forward. "This means you are choosing to make Jesus your Lord and Master, allowing Him to rule over your life. Do you understand?"

Cariana nodded, along with the others.

The pastor continued, "Do you believe in your heart that God raised Jesus from the dead?"

"Yes, sir," Cariana replied, her voice steady with conviction.

"And do you?" he asked another. "Do you believe God raised Jesus from the dead?"

"Yes, sir," came the response.

"Then," the pastor explained, "if you truly believe, the Holy Spirit will awaken your spirit, and you will be born again. This is the beginning of a new life in Christ."

The pastor paused, his eyes sweeping over those who had come forward. "This is not just a moment, but the start of a new journey," he said softly, his voice filled with compassion and certainty. "Salvation is more than just believing in your heart and confessing with your mouth—it's about choosing to live differently. It's about allowing Jesus to be the center of everything in your life. He becomes your Savior and your Lord. He transforms your heart, your mind, and your actions."

He looked directly at Cariana, who felt the weight of his words sink deep into her spirit. "When you receive the Holy Spirit, your old life is gone, and you are made new in Christ. This new life is not something you achieve on your own—it is God's gift to you, given freely through His grace."

Cariana's hands, which had trembled when she first raised them, were now steady, her palms open in surrender. She had struggled for so long with feelings of inadequacy and doubt, but standing there, she knew without a doubt that she was ready to embrace what God had for her. It was as if a door had opened in her heart, and she was stepping through it into a new reality—a reality where the past no longer had a hold on her, where hope was real, and where her future was secure in the hands of a loving God.

The pastor continued, "The Holy Spirit will guide you, empower you, and be your comforter. You will not be alone in this new life. God will be with you every step of the way, strengthening you to live according to His will."

As the pastor spoke, Cariana's thoughts were quiet but full of understanding. She knew, without a doubt, that this was the moment her life had been leading to. She was ready to make Jesus her Lord, to walk with Him, and to receive the new life He was offering. Her heart swelled with gratitude, and she silently prayed, *Lord, I'm ready. I'm ready to be made new in You.*

The pastor smiled warmly, sensing the sincerity in Cariana's heart. He raised his hand and led them in a prayer, a prayer of surrender, faith, and transformation. "Lord Jesus," he began, "we thank

You for these souls who have responded to Your call. We thank You for their belief in You, for the confession of their faith, and for the new life You are bringing them into today. Holy Spirit, we ask that You fill their hearts and minds with Your presence, that they may walk in Your strength and grace from this day forward."

As the prayer continued, Cariana repeated the words after the pastor, her voice full of assurance and hope: "Lord Jesus, I believe in my heart that You are Lord. I confess with my mouth that You are my Savior. Thank You for forgiving my sins and for making me new. I surrender my life to You, and I accept the new life You've given me. Help me to live for You every day. In Your name, I pray. Amen."

The pastor's voice was filled with joy as he concluded, "You are now a new creation in Christ. Welcome to the family of God."

Cariana felt the weight of those words settle over her, and for the first time in a long time, she felt truly free. It wasn't just about forgiveness—it was about a new identity, a new purpose, and a new hope. She was no longer the person she used to be. She was now a daughter of the King.

As the congregation erupted in praise and worship, Cariana's heart soared with the joy of salvation. She could feel the Holy Spirit moving within her, and a peace unlike any she had ever known filled her soul.

God had just begun a work in her, and she couldn't wait to see where this new journey would take her.

She wiped the tears from her eyes, her heart overwhelmed with gratitude and love for the Savior who had just given her a new beginning. She knew that life would not always be easy, but with Jesus at the center, she was ready to face whatever came next. As the choir's voices lifted once more in praise, Cariana lifted her hands to join them. This time, her voice was not just a quiet whisper—it was a bold, joyful proclamation of her new life in Christ. *Thank You, Jesus!* she whispered, her heart overflowing with gratitude. God was about to do something extraordinary in her life, and she was ready to witness it.

Chapter 12: Worship and Renewed Joy

The worship continued with an intensity that seemed to reach heaven itself. The pastor returned to the stage, gently asking the choir to sing softly. "Before you leave here today," he said, his voice carrying over the reverberating echoes of the congregation's praises, "remember that Jesus is about to do something big in your life. Whatever the enemy may bring, trust that everything happens for a reason. 'All things work together for good to them that love God, to them who are the called according to His purpose' (Romans 8:28, KJV)."

The words settled deep within Cariana's heart, like a seed planted in fertile soil. She could almost feel the weight of their truth, the assurance that everything she had been through, everything yet to come, was a part of God's perfect plan. Her mind traced back to the challenging moments she had faced—those moments where the pain seemed unending—and yet, standing there in the midst of this beautiful service, she felt a sense of peace. God was working, even when she couldn't see it.

With a final prayer over the congregation, the pastor dismissed them, but the worship persisted. The choir's voices swelled again, joined by the congregation's, lifting them all into a collective

moment of pure adoration. It was as if the whole church had become a vessel for praise, celebrating the goodness of God with all their hearts. Cariana felt caught up in that moment, her spirit soaring with the music, her joy a reflection of the healing she knew was beginning within her.
Cariana and Sara left the church service bursting with excitement, still humming the choir's song as they danced out of the building, arms linked. The joy from the service lingered, and the pastor's words echoed in their minds, a melody that wouldn't leave. Cariana couldn't stop smiling, her face lit up by the warmth of the sun and the newfound hope that filled her heart.

"'And we know that all things work together for good to them that love God, to them who are the called according to sHis purpose,'" Cariana recited, her voice full of conviction, as if claiming that promise for herself. "I'm called! Hmm... I wonder what my calling is. Like, what does God have for me?"
Sara nodded eagerly, her own excitement bubbling over. "Me too! I can't wait to figure out what God's purpose is for me. I feel like we're on the edge of something big—like this is just the beginning."

As they walked, laughing and replaying the

highlights of the message, the vibrant energy from the service still carried them forward. The sunlight warmed their backs, casting long shadows on the pavement as they made their way through the quiet neighborhood. Sara's phone rang suddenly, pulling them back to the present. It was her mom, asking them to stop by the grocery store and pick up a few things for dinner. They agreed without hesitation, happy to run the errand as they continued chatting about everything that had just happened.

Cariana, still in awe of how the service had moved her, said, "I can't wait to tell my mom what the pastor said. It felt like he was talking directly to me. Like, everything he said resonated so deeply, you know?"

Sara grinned. "Same! Especially that part about walking with a purpose. I feel like something big is coming, like God is about to do something amazing in our lives. I'm just waiting for it to unfold."

The conversation shifted as they entered the grocery store, the automatic doors opening with a soft swoosh. The cool air inside was a stark contrast to the warm afternoon, and the faint scent of fresh produce filled the space. Sara glanced at Cariana and asked, "So, are you ready for summer school?"

Cariana sighed but smiled, trying to mask her nerves. "Not really. I mean, its summer, right? I was hoping for a break, but I guess I have to catch up on all the stuff I missed. It's not going to be easy, but I'm excited for tenth grade. At least it's the last summer school I'll have to do." She paused, her voice quieter as she thought back to the tough time she'd had, the emotional weight still heavy in her chest. "I... you know, I have to go to summer school because I missed a few classes at the end of ninth grade... you know, because of the incident."

The words were soft, barely above a whisper. Her mind flitted to that painful memory—those final weeks of ninth grade when everything had spiraled out of control. Her life had been turned upside down in the wake of the incident, and school had been the last place she felt safe. The dark cloud of shame and guilt had lingered for what felt like an eternity, and her absence from school had been a reflection of her inner turmoil. But now, standing in the grocery store with Sara, the future felt a little less daunting.

Sara, sensing the shift in Cariana's mood, gave her a reassuring smile. "I know you've been through a lot but look at you now. You're so strong, Cariana.

You're going to make it through, I just know it."

Cariana's lips curved into a grateful smile, a soft chuckle escaping her. "Thanks, Sara. I'm trying. I'm really trying." She lifted her head, ready to face the summer ahead, a quiet but steady sense of determination filling her. Something in her was changing, and with each step she took, she was moving closer to the person God had called her to be.

Chapter 13: The Pursuit

The girls pushed the shopping cart down the bright, fluorescent-lit aisles, laughing as they discussed their plans for the upcoming school year. Cariana and Sara exchanged excited thoughts about new classes, teachers, and which friends they were hoping to have in their homerooms. The cool air of the store mixed with the comforting scent of fresh produce, but their conversation was interrupted when they reached the meat section.

Cariana placed her purse into the cart, thinking she could focus on choosing the right cuts of meat. As Sara grabbed a pack of chicken, Cariana leaned over, inspecting the options. Out of the corner of her eye, she noticed a boy pacing back and forth near their cart, his hands shoved in his pockets. She barely gave him a second thought, still caught up in the banter with Sara. The store was busy, and she figured he was just another shopper on his own, looking for something.

But then, as they walked further away from the cart, she saw him move closer. Her stomach churned with an unexplainable unease. Just as Sara reached for a package of steaks, the boy, quick as a flash, darted toward the cart, snatching Cariana's purse with a jerk that sent it tumbling to the floor.

Before either of them could react, the boy sprinted past them, his footsteps echoing through the store as Cariana's purse swung in his hand. The silver clasp glinted in the harsh store lights. Panic surged through Cariana's chest, and without thinking, she shouted, "He's got my purse!"

Sara's eyes went wide with shock, but instinct took over. "Thief!" she yelled, her voice loud and sharp. The girls dashed after the boy, weaving between displays and startled shoppers. Their shoes skidded on the polished floor, and Cariana's heart pounded in her ears as the sound of their hurried steps mingled with the boy's rapid pace.

They rounded corners, their breath coming in ragged gasps, but the boy was fast—too fast. With every step, the gap between them widened. Cariana's desperation grew. Her hand reached out, but she was just too far away. Then, in an instant, he shot out the automatic sliding doors and disappeared into the parking lot, vanishing as quickly as he'd arrived.

Out of breath, Cariana came to a sudden halt. Her chest heaved, and she turned to look back at the store entrance, her eyes wide in disbelief. The parking lot was empty. No sign of him, no one had even tried to stop him. Her purse was gone. Her money, her ID, and everything that made her feel secure gone in a flash.

Sara was panting beside her, shaking her head in disbelief. "That—he—how did no one stop him?" she said, the words coming out in a disbelieving whisper.

Cariana's knees buckled for a second as the weight of the situation hit her all at once. She felt exposed, violated, and utterly helpless. Her heart pounded as the tears threatened to spill over. It wasn't just about the money—it was about the feeling of being watched and taken advantage of, like everything she had trusted was now gone.

They quickly found the store manager, who seemed as stunned as they were. He immediately called the police, his voice steady, though his face betrayed his concern. He ushered them to the back office, where he pulled up the security footage, hoping to catch a glimpse of the thief's face.

The video showed the boy clearly—his hoodie pulled tight over his head, his movements quick and deliberate. He grabbed the purse with practiced ease, slipping it from the cart and bolting for the door. But, when the manager zoomed in on his face, they found that he was unrecognizable, just a blur of features.

The officer on the phone with the manager confirmed that a police unit would arrive soon, but Cariana didn't know how much comfort that brought. She just kept replaying the moment in her mind—her purse gone, the boy's swift exit, and the apathy of everyone around her.

Cariana's hands were shaking as she dialed her mom's number, her voice cracking when her mom answered.

"Mom," she sobbed into the phone, her words tumbling out in a rush, "someone stole my purse! It's all gone—my money, my ID, everything..." The reality of the theft crashed over her in waves, and the tears that had been building up finally spilled over.

"I'm so sorry, honey," her mom said, her voice tight with worry. "Stay there. I'll be there as soon as I can. Don't worry, we'll take care of it."

But in that moment, it didn't feel like anything could take care of the empty, heavy feeling in her chest. Her purse wasn't just a bag—it was her sense of security, her connection to her life outside the store. And now, it was gone, slipping through her fingers in a moment of shocking speed.

Chapter 14: The Bigger Picture

Her mom tried to calm her down, but Cariana couldn't shake the feeling of helplessness. After she hung up, her mind raced back to the pastor's words from the service: *I'm walking with a purpose*. She wanted to believe that everything happening to her was part of God's plan, but it didn't feel like it right now. She could still hear the echo of her mom's worried voice on the phone, but it faded as the tears started to fall. Everything felt so out of control.

"How is this working for my good?" she whispered to herself, wiping away her tears. "Everything bad keeps happening to me." It felt like one thing after another. She had tried so hard to make the right choices, to follow the path that she thought would lead to something better, and yet it all seemed to be unraveling.

Sensing her friend's despair, Sara put a hand on her shoulder, her touch grounding Cariana, even just a little. "I know it feels unfair, but remember what the pastor said? Even in the bad times, God is with us. Maybe there's something we can't see right now, but He's working things out for your good. Just trust Him."

Cariana nodded slowly, though feeling comforted in that moment was hard. There was a part of her that wanted to believe it, but another part was struggling to hold on to hope. "It's just... I feel like I'm trying so hard to do the right thing, and then this happens. Why does it feel like something knocks me back every time I take a step forward?"

Sara gave her a gentle smile, her eyes full of empathy. "Maybe it's because you're getting closer to something bigger than you think. The enemy always fights hardest when God's about to do something great in your life."

The weight of Sara's words lingered in the air, though Cariana couldn't quite wrap her mind around them. How could this moment of pain possibly lead to something bigger? How could this feel like anything other than the end of a long, difficult road? But despite herself, Cariana wiped her eyes again and took a deep breath, trying to steady herself. "Yeah, maybe you're right. It's just hard to see it right now."

They finished up the police report, the task feeling almost trivial compared to the heaviness that hung over Cariana's heart. The routine details of the day seemed out of place against the backdrop of her overwhelming emotions. Afterward, they left the store, the cool breeze of the evening brushing against their skin as they stepped outside. The weight of the day still lingered in Cariana's chest, the sense of loss, the uncertainty.

But as they walked back to Sara's house, something shifted, however small it might have been. In the quiet of the walk, Cariana silently prayed, asking God to help her believe that He was still working, even in this moment of loss. She didn't have all the answers, and maybe she never would, but she needed to trust that God was still there, still moving in her life. *Please help me believe,* she thought, her heart desperate for peace.

The words from Romans 8:28 played over in her mind, a soft reminder that she clung to with a mixture of hope and doubt: *All things work together for good...* Maybe, just maybe, this was part of something bigger, something she couldn't see yet. Maybe she wasn't just walking aimlessly in her pain. Maybe, just maybe, there was a purpose even in the hardest moments.

With that thought, Cariana's resolve started to shift. She still didn't have it all figured out, and the tears still stung her eyes, but she decided that she would keep walking. She would keep walking, even through the tears, trusting that God was leading her to something she couldn't understand yet, but that He knew. She wasn't alone in her struggle, and despite the hurt, she wasn't without hope. She would continue to walk, one step at a time.

Sara walked beside her, the steady presence of her friend a reminder that even in her darkest moments, she wasn't truly alone. And so, Cariana took another step, and then another, holding on to the words that had once seemed like distant comfort but were starting to feel like lifelines. "God, I trust you," she whispered softly under her breath. "Even when it hurts, I trust you."

The weight of the day was still there, but it didn't feel quite as heavy now. As they walked on, the evening sky above them deepened into twilight, and Cariana felt a glimmer of hope stirring in her heart. Maybe it wasn't about seeing the end of the road. Maybe it was about trusting the journey, trusting that God was leading her somewhere, somewhere good, even if it was hard to see it right now. She could trust that. And with each step, she would keep walking, one step closer to the purpose He had for her.

To be continued......

To anyone who has faced the unimaginable pain of molestation or assault, know this: you are not alone, and you are not defined by what has happened to you. The journey to healing is not easy, but you have a strength within you that no one can take away. Through Jesus, you have the strength to overcome, and He is here with you every step of the way. There is hope beyond the hurt, a future beyond the fear.

No matter how dark it may feel, light still exists. Every step you take, no matter how small, is a victory. You are resilient, and your life has purpose. Hold onto hope, lean into your faith, and allow yourself to heal at your own pace. Never give up because brighter days are ahead. You are worthy of love, peace, and freedom.

Broken, But Healed

I once walked with shattered steps,
pieces of me scattered, left—
a heart weighed down by silent cries,
a soul that lived in hollow skies.

The nights were long, the days unkind,
memories tangled in my mind.
I built my walls, I hid my pain,
fearing I'd never rise again.

But healing whispered in the dark,
a flicker first, then full of spark.
Hope stretched out its gentle hands,
guiding me to solid land.

The past still lingers, but it's light,
no longer drowning me in night.
Scars remain, but they don't bleed—
they tell a story, plant a seed.

I was broken, but now I stand,
no longer fragile, firm in hand.
Not who I was, yet more complete—
stronger now on steady feet.

I learned that wounds don't steal my worth,
they shape the soul, they birth rebirth.
Each tear that fell, each ache inside,
became the place where strength resides.

I do not fear the storms ahead,
I've danced in rain and risen instead.

What once destroyed has made me whole,
etching wisdom in my soul.

So if you find yourself undone,
lost in darkness, far from sun,
know the breaking isn't the end—
it's where you learn to rise again.

Continue the Journey

Thank you for reading The Life of a Fighter. This is just the beginning of an unfolding story of strength, resilience, and purpose. To follow the journey, continue with I'm Walking with a Purpose, where the path becomes more challenging yet more meaningful.

The story further unfolds in Unforgiveness and, ultimately, reaches new horizons in A New Beginning. Each installment reveals new insights, challenges, and personal victories through struggle, growth, and a spiritual walk, making this series a complete journey of transformation and hope. May this series bless every reader along the way.

Thank you for taking this journey with me.

www.ingramcontent.com/pod-product-compliance
Lightning Source LLC
Chambersburg PA
CBHW040156160726
48006CB00014B/1770